ENTERING THE
TEEN ZONE

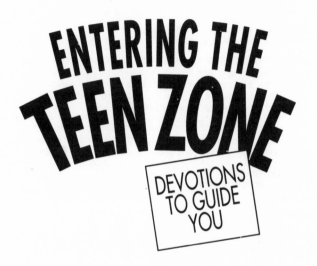

ENTERING THE
TEEN ZONE

DEVOTIONS
TO GUIDE
YOU

William L. Coleman

AUGSBURG **MINNEAPOLIS**

ENTERING THE TEEN ZONE
Devotions to Guide You

Scripture quotations unless otherwise noted are from the Holy Bible: New International Version. Copyright 1978 by the New York International Bible Society. Used by permission of Zondervan Bible Publishers.

Cover design: Hilber Nelson
Cover illustration: John P. Hanson

Library of Congress Cataloging-in-Publication Data

Coleman, William L.
    Entering the teen zone : devotions to guide you / William L. Coleman.
        p.   cm.
    Summary: Uses passages and quotations from Scripture to help guide Christian teens through the sometimes anxious and confusing period of adolescence.
    ISBN 0-8066-2499-X
    1. Teenagers—Prayer-books and devotions—English. 2. Teenagers—Conduct of life. 3. Christian life—1960– [1. Prayer books and devotions. 2. Christian life. 3. Conduct of life.] I. Title.
BV4850.C5646   1990
242'.63—dc20   90-43092
                                                         CIP
                                                          AC

The paper used in this publication meets the minimum requirements of American National Standard for Information Sciences— Permanence of Paper for Printed Library Materials, ANSI Z329.48–1984.

Manufactured in the U.S.A.   AF 9-2499

94   93   92   4   5   6   7   8   9   10

Contents

A Note to
the Reader

School may have seemed long until now, but life should start to take off soon. Changes are coming fast. Some of them are exciting and good. A few changes are scary and confusing.

Have fun being a teenager. There is plenty to enjoy and accomplish and tons of great people to meet. I think God is just as enthused about these years as you are.

BILL COLEMAN

Thanks!

A special thanks to the young people who discussed these subjects with me. Their outlook on life is a great lift.

I also want to express my appreciation to Mary Coleman who worked extensively on collecting material and furnishing guidance.

The Anti-Boredom Squad

"There's nothing to do."

How many times have you heard a whining child say that? There were plenty of things to do, but the child just wanted to complain. When children are idle for a few minutes, they often turn to their parents and demand that something be done to "entertain" them.

Aren't you glad you aren't that young anymore? As a teenager you are a take-charge person. You have an adult mind. You can create your own life and find a great deal to get involved in.

Yet you still hear teens say, "There's nothing to do."

Actually, the statement is inaccurate. There is more than enough to do. What the person is really saying is, "There isn't anything I feel like doing."

A 13-year-old boy in the suburbs of Chicago groaned those famous words, "There's nothing to do." If he had stopped to think, these were the facts:

♦ His bedroom looked liked Dracula's vault.

♦ His friend, Jered, would have loved to play tennis with him.

♦ There was a history test the next day.

♦ There was a youth meeting in 30 minutes.

♦ He knew a classmate originally from Laos who needed help with her English.

♦ His father would pass out if he stacked the woodpile.

♦ Kevin was always bugging him to play video games.

With all of this and more, the 13-year-old sat in the living room like mold on cheese and howled, "There's

11

nothing to do." It was as if he expected members of "The Anti-Boredom Squad" to come rushing into the room. Frantically they would pick him up off the couch, bounce him around in the air, and then tickle him under the arms to get him laughing. They would then rush him to a waiting fire truck outside and begin driving him around town while they fed him ice cream and cake as sirens wailed.

Most of us dream of an "Anti-Boredom Squad." But that's kind of like the Easter Bunny. The fact is, there are tons of interesting, challenging, fulfilling things to do—if we want to do them.

People who sit around idly complaining soon become a pain to themselves and to everyone else. Whining looks ugly whether it is on a child, a teenager, an adult, or a grandparent. Idleness hurts everybody. Smart people get involved. Dorks just groan and moan.

> *"Besides, they get into the habit of being idle and going about from house to house. And not only do they become idlers, but also gossips and busybodies, saying things they ought not to."*
>
> *1 Timothy 5:13*

Keep thinking

1. If you are bored, what do you usually do to snap out of it?
2. How long has it been since you whined, "There's nothing to do?"
3. Who can you call when it seems like there's nothing to do?

The Popularity Trap

When you become a teenager, your social life becomes complicated. Usually you go to a new school where you are thrown in with a bunch of new people and separated from your old friends. You aren't sure where you will end up in the big shuffle.

As all this happens, your head might spin and you could get fairly nervous about the situation.

But no need to worry. Stay calm. The earth might shake a little, but it won't fall apart. Keep a few guidelines in mind.

First, it's smart to keep a few of your old friends. That might not be easy. You may be in different classes, you may join separate activities, you might be eating during different lunch hours. Whatever the circumstances, it's worth the work to hold on to a few of yesterday's friends.

The people who have known you for a long time can be a big help when you make decisions. They can tell you if you are starting to hang around with the wrong crowd. Old friends know if your attitude is turning bad. They also can encourage you when they see you making the right moves.

Young people who go into a new setting and cut themselves off or who get lost in the shuffle often have a tough time making the transition. Add new friends, but don't let all of the old ones get away.

Also, don't fall for the popularity trap. There are some teens who think they must have 300 friends. Working hard to be popular can cause you to do some dumb things you will regret later.

The happiest teenagers seem to be the ones who find a circle of close friends. They treat those friends well. They share together, laugh together, worry together, and sometimes they confront each other when they are wrong. Their friends are people who have the same set of high values and morals. Good friends don't drag each other down; they lift each other up.

If a young person collects 20 friends or 100, that's OK because it's good to act friendly. But the friends to aim for, the friends to keep in touch with, are the close ones.

The popularity trap can hurt a person. When you need someone you can count on when the going gets tough, it's your close friends who come through and not the big crowd.

Do something for your friends. Call them up. Get together. See how they are getting along. Help them when you can. It's the close friends who really count.

"Do not forsake your friend."

Proverbs 27:10

Keep thinking

1. Who are two or three friends you especially like and want to keep?
2. What could you do today to keep in touch with those friends?

The Top 10

Has any of this ever happened to you?

♦ Have you ever tried to read the Bible during breakfast only to fall asleep and drop your head into your oatmeal?

♦ Have you ever been reading the Bible and gotten the 12 disciples confused with the 12 tribes of Israel?

♦ Do you ever wonder if it was Solomon and Beersheba, David and Beersheba, Samson and Beersheba, or Beersheba and the seven dwarfs?

If you are afraid of the Bible because it is all too confusing, let's step back and look at it again. The entire Bible looks too big and has too many characters to swallow all at once.

For the beginning Bible reader, here is a list of the top 10 easy-to-understand passages of Scripture. Don't try to figure out Zechariah, Zephaniah, and Zerubbabel. Start by looking at a few of these easy-to-read, practical chapters in the Bible. Read them slowly, a little each day. Think them over and see what they mean for your life.

The Top 10 for Beginners
(not necessarily in this order)

1. The Ten Commandments (Exodus 20:1-17)
2. Story of the Prodigal Son (Luke 15:11-32)
3. The Sermon on the Mount (Matthew 5, 6, 7)
4. Resurrection of Jesus Christ (John 20:1-9)
5. The Love Chapter (1 Corinthians 13)

6. Daniel Making Decisions (Daniel 1)
7. How to Handle Anxiety (Philippians 4:1-9)
8. Parent-Child Relationship (Ephesians 6:1-4)
9. Story of the Rich Fool (Luke 12:13-21)
10. The Good Samaritan (Luke 10:25-37)

The Bible is packed with great stories and practical help if you know where to look.

Keep thinking

1. Which of the top 10 do you think you would most enjoy reading?
2. When will be a good time for you to begin?

Passing Notes

All of us have done it. We have passed notes around a classroom. Maybe we wanted to find out who won the game last night, or we wonder if Jennifer is going to The Pizza Pit after school. Sometimes notes whistle past between a boyfriend and a girlfriend—especially if they're arguing. A few times a note goes wandering around during a test when someone is frantically trying to find out who won the Civil War.

How often have you found a note stuffed through the air vents in your locker? Have you ever discovered a note crammed in your gym shoes?

Recently I learned a new use for this age-old form of communication. I have started to write notes to God. I don't stuff them in lunch bags or slip them in anyone's coat pocket, but I do enjoy writing them.

My problem is concentration. It seems like the minute I begin talking to God, my mind runs off in every direction. I think about what I have to do an hour from now or where I am going tonight or whatever.

But when I write to God, I concentrate better. I don't have to worry about spelling or punctuation. No one else will read my notes, and I figure God won't get upset at a split infinitive or a slightly misdirected preposition.

This isn't a diary. After writing for a few weeks I throw the notes away. The process has given me freedom to talk to God. Most mornings I write a note to my heavenly Father. I tell God how I feel, what I need, what I want for others, how great God is. Whatever. I make up my own rules as I go along. The next day I may do it differently.

I never sit and agonize over what I might say or what I should say. I merely pick up a pen, use an old notebook, and say what is on my heart. There is no need to mail what I write; I think God has a personal fax machine.

This may not work for everyone. Nothing ever does. But it means a great deal to be able to jot off a note to God.

> *"After he had dismissed them, he went up into the hills by himself to pray."*
>
> *Matthew 14:23*

Keep thinking

1. When do you enjoy talking to God?
2. What do you talk to God about?

Feeling Like a Hypocrite

Suppose you convinced everyone you were an eagle. Your friends would probably be impressed. They most likely have never met and talked to a majestic bird like you.

One of the first things they might ask is for the chance to see you fly. Eagles can soar in beautiful silent patterns, and your friends will be anxious to watch you run along the ground and take off.

At first you would probably bluff a great deal. You'd say you had a sore wing one day. The next day you would claim you had a cold and heights made you dizzy.

After a week or two of making up phony excuses, everyone would catch on to the facts. You aren't an eagle and never have been one.

You have been a hypocrite. You claimed to be something you were not.

But suppose you claimed to be a Christian. Does that make you a hypocrite, too?

That depends.

If you say you are perfect because you are a Christian, then your friends will soon see that isn't true. If you insist that you are better than others because you are a Christian, your friends will know you aren't telling the truth.

A hypocrite is someone who claims to be something he or she is not.

The word *hypocrite* was first used to describe actors who wore masks to cover up who they really were. If I wear a mask to pretend I am someone else, I am a hypocrite.

But if I claim to be a Christian and still do wrong things, I am not a hypocrite. Christians made mistakes, do wrong things, and sin. We make no claim to be perfect.

You can go to church, read your Bible, and pray, and still mess up. That doesn't make you a hypocrite. All Christians mess up. But as Christians we try to resist sin.

Some of us are afraid that others will call us hypocrites. They won't if they understand the Christian life. We aren't perfect, but we do try not to mess up.

Relax. If you try to follow Jesus Christ, you are no hypocrite.

> "You hypocrite, first take the plank out of your own eye, and then you will see clearly to remove the speck from your brother's eye."
>
> Matthew 7:5

Keep thinking

1. Do you ever find yourself bragging about your Christianity?
2. Do you see yourself as a humble Christian trying to help others?

Huffing and Puffing

Jackie bustled into Megan's bedroom, huffing and puffing. Megan looked up to see her older sister standing over her, snorting like a hyperactive dragon.

"You have some nerve, you twerp," Jackie ranted.

"What happened now?" Megan asked calmly. "The cat eat your eye makeup?"

"Don't get smart with me. This is Mom's fault for spoiling you." Jackie thrust her hands on her hips.

"Oh, yeah, *I'm* spoiled all right."

"How could you wear that dumb monster sweatshirt to school? You look like a third grader with that goofy thing on."

"You mean you're mad because of what I wore to school today? I don't believe this." Megan tossed her pencil on top of her open books.

"I knew you wouldn't understand, but Jason, the guy I'm trying desperately to get a date with, came up to me in study hall and said, 'What's your little sister—a monster freak?' I could have died."

"Well, don't let me stop you." Megan grunted as she picked up her pencil and went back to her homework.

Have you ever had a scene like this at your house? Has your brother or sister ever popped up from nowhere and started chewing you out for no reason? When was the last time you and your parents swapped words in a hot argument?

Arguing is common in families. Some do it without words. They slam doors, stomp down the hall, or fold their arms, lock their jaws, and stare out the window.

Other families throw words around like grenades. They toss accusations in every direction, call someone a couple of choice names, and get everyone upset.

Have you ever wondered about your family's disagreements? Does the arguing bother you? Have you thought maybe your family is not like everybody else's?

If your family is like the ones just described, you probably have a normal household. All of us argue either silently or vocally. It doesn't mean we hate each other. It just means that people can't always agree.

When people get mean, however, it can be a serious problem. When family members start smacking each other around or parents tell their children to get out, then it might be time to get some outside help. You might talk to a school counselor or a minister.

The disciples were close followers of Jesus. They tried hard to do what they felt he wanted them to do. But they still managed to quarrel from time to time.

A hot argument may not always be the best, but it sounds fairly normal.

"An argument started among the disciples as to which of them would be the greatest."
Luke 9:46

Keep thinking

1. What do you and your parents argue about most? What do you and your brothers and sisters argue about most?
2. What can you do to cut down on arguments at home?
3. Would you like to talk to a school counselor or a minister about arguing at your house?

Pizza Stuffers

What do you like on your pizza? Do you order pepperoni sprinkled over extra cheese? Or do you enjoy those dark lumps of hamburger with mushrooms dotted all around? Maybe you are an anchovy freak or you want Canadian bacon or possibly tiny shrimp lying in every direction waiting to be gobbled up.

But why mess around? Get everything on your pizza and don't settle for the thin variety. Order a thick pizza with stringy cheese pulling from piece to piece.

How many slices of pizza can you stuff down at one sitting? If no one is watching, can you pork out with three, four, or even five pieces? What is the most pizza you have ever eaten in one sitting?

Most of us enjoy pizza and probably could eat it for nearly every meal.

When you become a teenager, there is something else you might begin to enjoy almost as much as pizza. It's called gossip. Since you are no longer a child, your social world becomes more complicated. You become more intrigued by other people and their personal lives.

Most teens want to know who likes whom, who isn't talking to whom, and who lied about a friend. Young people are fascinated by what other people are up to. An increased interest in the social lives of others leads to more talk about people, and more talk about people leads to more gossip.

And gossip is like pizza. The more you eat the more you want. Eventually we stuff ourselves with gossip.

Gossip is not just talking. Gossip is saying something to make a person look bad. If you are spreading stories about people (true stories or false) to tear them down, you've done it—you are gossiping.

If you have ever been hurt by gossip, you know how painful it can be. Then why would anybody want to do it to somebody else? Because gossip is like pizza. We enjoy putting other people down. And like pizza, once we start, we find it hard to stop until we have stuffed ourselves.

There is a higher road to travel. You don't have to talk about others in a bad light. Once you start, it's tough to stop.

> *"The words of a gossip are like choice morsels;*
> *they go down to a man's inmost parts."*
> *Proverbs 26:22*

Keep thinking

1. Have you ever been a victim of gossip? How did it feel?
2. Why do we enjoy gossiping so much?

Feel Like Crying

When Aaron's parents divorced, he felt terrible. He loved both his mother and father and hated to see them go separate ways. Aaron knew nothing would ever be the same again.

Quietly, Aaron went to his room to sit and think. He wanted to be alone. Sadness gripped the teenager as his eyes welled up with water. Aaron was afraid to cry, so he fought the tears back.

After all, he figured, adults don't cry, and he was going to handle this like an adult. Aaron bit his lip, tried to swallow the lump in his throat, and stared at the wall.

Like many other young people, Aaron had lost something that was extremely important to him. The two people who meant the most to him weren't going to live together anymore. Just as bad, they weren't very nice to each other.

All of that hurt Aaron and he was trying to pretend it didn't bother him.

If you lose something you care about—a grandparent, a special friend, a pet, or whatever—what is wrong with crying? No matter if you are a male or a female, sometimes the best thing you can do is cry.

It doesn't mean you will cry every day for the rest of your life. Neither does it mean you will cry about everything. You don't have to weep when the leaves fall or when your cat comes home late or when the toast is burned.

But when you have lost something you deeply care about and you feel terrible, tears may be the best medicine.

When Jesus Christ felt deeply hurt, he cried. For him crying was necessary and natural. He didn't sob over the local athletic contests, but Jesus did cry when it mattered.

The Bible teaches us that we are blessed or helped if we can mourn. People who hold everything in become uptight and miserable. Smart people get sad, let it out, and find a way to go on with life. Some people who refuse to cry are sad forever.

None of us is looking to cry every day. But when the occasion calls for it, don't be afraid to let the tears flow.

"Blessed are those who mourn, for they will be comforted."

Matthew 5:4

Keep thinking

1. What kind of loss has made you want to cry?
2. Did you cry? Why or why not?
3. If you cried, how did you feel afterward?

Do My Parents Love Me?

"Nobody loves me around here."

With those words Kristen marched outside, slamming the door behind her. Confused and angry, she stomped down the front steps, books tucked tightly under one arm, clarinet case bobbing in the other hand.

Kristen was saying what most of us feel sometime and what many of us say sooner or later.

Kristen was wondering whether her parents really love her. It's a fair question, and Kristen deserves a straight answer. The answer is: almost certainly they love her. But some parents dislike their children. Not many, but a few. That's being honest.

But almost all parents seem to love their children. If our parents love us, there are some sure signs to look for. We can call it evidence. Just like when it rains, we expect things to be wet. If we see a duck, we expect it to quack.

There are two basic ways to show love:

1. We say we love each other.
2. We act as if we love each other.

For some of us the first way is the hardest. When we try to say "I love you," our tongue turns to leather and we just mumble. Life might go a little smoother if we could bring ourselves to say those magic words, but it takes some work.

The second method is tough but necessary. We need to act like we love somebody. This means we care what happens to him or her. When we can, we help by being encouraging, being close, pitching in and lending a hand. Love is as love does.

When our parents supply food, inquire about our health, buy clothes for us, and protect us, they *show* love. Parents who hurt, abuse, and abandon do not demonstrate love. Parents who draw lines and stop their children from hurting themselves also show love. They care.

This is God's approach to love. God said he loved us and God proved that love by sending Jesus to die for us. God does both parts well.

The fact that parents make rules doesn't mean they don't love you. Often rules mean they do love you.

Some parents are better at it than others. They may love as deeply but have trouble expressing that love. You can help your parents by taking the first big steps. If you go out of your way to show love, your parents might also find it easier to act in a loving way.

Too often parents and teens begin fighting and neither shows much love.

Check it out. Parents who do things for their children usually love them. If your parents don't do loving things, you may have to take the initiative and show your love first.

> *"Love is patient, love is kind. It does not envy,*
> *it does not boast, it is not proud. It is not rude,*
> *it is not self-seeking, it is not easily angered."*
> *1 Corinthians 13:4-5*

Keep thinking

1. How do you show love to your parents?
2. How do your parents show love to you?

Who Holds Your Net?

Have you ever seen footage of a terrible fire on the evening news? Usually the building is several stories high and smoke billows out the windows. The television camera focuses on a person sitting on the ledge, one leg in and one leg out. The person looks both ways, trying desperately to decide whether to jump or go back inside.

Maybe the decision would be easier if the person knew exactly who was holding the net. Are just two people holding it? If the person leaps out into space, are the rescuers strong enough to guarantee a safe landing? Are the people holding the net chicken? Will they all run when they see the person become airborne?

There's a lot to consider before you go sailing out of windows.

Every once in a while life gets extra tough. Troubles begin to pile up. You feel picked on, unappreciated, and useless. You might even feel a little like the person on the window ledge.

When you want to jump out and talk to someone, who is holding the net to catch you as you fall? Who can you depend on when you need somebody to listen?

Check out the following list. Out of those listed, who would you go to if you wanted to talk over a problem? If you needed a net, how many of these people would be able to hold it for you?

Friend   Minister
Parent   Neighbor

Teacher	Recreation director
Relative	Brother/sister
Counselor	Youth director
Someone else	God

You might be able to check some on the list twice because there may be more than one friend or teacher you can count on.

While life is often good, life can also carry a miserable stinger. When the sting hurts, it helps to talk to someone.

Teens who feel they have no one to talk to find life much harder. They may let the pressure build up inside, or they could fly off the handle and do something goofy.

Each of us needs a few people who can listen—some net holders. The net holders are around, and they are willing to help. It would be a shame if we fouled up because we forgot to reach out to people we can count on.

> *"Plans fail for lack of counsel, but with many advisers they succeed."*
>
> *Proverbs 15:22*

Keep thinking

1. If you needed someone to talk to right now, who could you go to at school?
2. Who among your relatives is a particularly good net holder?

Is There a Rebel
Hiding In You?

No one was going to tell Ryan what to do. He had decided early in life to be Mr. Cool and nobody could stop him. Drinking, skipping school, lying, and stealing were high on Ryan's list as he tried to prove that he could do anything he wanted.

The idea of being a rebel sounded good to Ryan. He didn't have to do what his parents told him, and he worked hard at trying to fool his teachers. If anyone said Ryan had to do something, his first thought was, "You're going to have to make me." Immediately he would begin thinking of a way to get out of it.

Most people liked Ryan. He was fun to talk to and even exciting to be with. Friends could always count on him to think of adventurous ways to get around the rules. But over the years, some people began to resent Ryan's behavior. Adults and teens alike started to grow tired of his rebellion. He was going too far too often.

Eventually Ryan's problems came to a head in a hardware store on a Saturday afternoon. After looking both ways to make sure the clerk was busy, Ryan piled four packs of batteries in his coat pocket and moved quickly out the side door. No sooner had he stepped on the pavement than a large hand grabbed his arm. Ryan turned his head to stare directly into the eyes of an angry security officer.

Many of us want to rebel. We want to be ourselves, express our own personalities, find out who we are. We don't want someone else building boxes for us and then demanding that we stay in them. I want to be me. You want to be you. That sounds normal.

But there is a time when rebellion goes too far. There is a line we cross where we begin to hurt others and hurt ourselves. At that point we are no longer trying to find out who we are. At that point we have started doing evil. Hurting ourselves and hurting others is wrong and sinful.

When we cross the line and do harm, someone needs to stop us. A parent, a teacher, a police officer—maybe all three. If we can't control ourselves, someone else must control us. That's the way life has to work.

Go ahead and rebel. Wear orange socks. Hang the pictures upside down in your bedroom. Put chocolate topping on your fried chicken. Spit into the wind if you have to. But don't go nuts. Don't cross the line and do what is evil.

> *"An evil man is bent only on rebellion; a merciless official will be sent against him."*
> Proverbs 17:11

Keep thinking

1. What would you like to do that your parents do not approve of?
2. Have you talked to them about it?
3. Can you think of another approach?

How Popular Am I?

Jill decided that she would become popular. Everyone would know who she was. She wanted to be recognized and accepted by as many people as possible.

At the first opportunity, Jill ran for class president. She made posters, had a few students working on her campaign, and even made a short speech in front of the class.

Finally election day came and Jill sat nervously waiting for the results at the end of the last period. Mrs. Beacher announced the final votes:

Brad—32
Jill—20
Angie—16

Jill smiled at all her friends as they left the room. She even went over and congratulated Brad on his victory. But behind her stiff lip was a teenager who hurt and wanted to cry.

Instead of being popular, Jill felt like a total loser. She felt rejected and disliked.

Like many of us, Jill thought she needed lots of people to tell her she was all right. Unless bus loads of friends hugged and praised her, Jill figured she must be the number one hair ball of all time.

What Jill needed to learn was that crowds come and go. The person who is surrounded by a dozen friends today could be all alone and feeling blue later tonight. Crowds aren't where the real friends are. She also needed to know that a handful of good people are far more important than 100 people she barely knows.

Fortunately, Jill is learning about groups and crowds. Even though someone else won the election, she knows her life can go on quite well.

Some people never learn that. Some teens and even adults keep kicking themselves because they didn't become homecoming queen or cheerleader or team captain or whatever. Jill got over that feeling and realized how much her close friends really meant to her.

A great many people crowded themselves around Jesus Christ. They liked to watch the miracles, listen to the stories, and share the friendship with others.

One day Jesus taught some hard lessons. He talked about a new life that the Spirit of God gives. He told them that the physical things we see are not what is really important.

When the large group heard that, some of them became upset and left. They didn't want to be followers anymore.

What did Jesus do then? Did he sulk, pout, tell himself no one liked him? No, Jesus knew that crowds come and go. He didn't give up. He continued his teaching. And he was surrounded by his faithful friends. It's the small circle of friends that really counts.

> *"From this time many of his disciples turned back and no longer followed him."*
>
> *John 6:66*

Keep thinking

1. Do you ever think the captain of the team or the class president is better than you? Why?
2. Name five friends you enjoy spending time with.

Fear of Fatness

Don't you get tired of hearing about it? Every other ad on television seems to tell us how to lose weight. Articles in magazines spell out the evils of eating too much. After a while you feel like the only safe things to eat are tree bark and barley oats.

Weight loss has become a national obsession. Emphasis on the perfect body has caused some teenagers to worry about fat all the time, and their attempts at losing weight range from ridiculous to destructive.

Before getting caught up in the latest fad, try to aim for these three goals. Each of these is more important than being skinny.

1. Stay active
2. Stay healthy
3. Stay alert

Refrigerator lizards are bound to put on weight. People who lean toward an active life-style tend to remain thinner. Life-style can be lifelong. If we enjoy physical activity, those interests will probably carry over into adulthood.

The second goal is to stay healthy. Be more concerned about blood pressure and cholesterol than actual size. Some people seem to handle more weight than others. The basic question is whether or not we are doing damage to our bodies.

Our third goal is to stay awake mentally. If we are sluggish and dull, we might be eating too much of the wrong things.

We don't all need to look alike or be the same size, but we do need to be as healthy as reasonably possible. If that is our goal, our weight may take care of itself.

God is interested in our soul both for now and forever. God is also concerned about our health. Good health makes now a lot more fun.

> *"Dear friend, I pray that you may enjoy good health and that all may go well with you, even as your soul is getting along well."*
>
> 3 John 2

Keep thinking

1. How would you describe your life-style?
   a. active
   b. kind of active
   c. dead fish
2. What are two steps you could take immediately to improve your health?

Be Happy!

Happy people and unhappy people are all the same. Both of them:

♦ Step on chewing gum.
♦ Lose their homework.
♦ Burp at awkward times.
♦ Watch their last quarter roll under the pop machine.
♦ Wash a contact lens down the drain.
♦ Double dribble.
♦ Raise their hand and forget what they were going to say.

We all have the same kinds of experiences. Happy people drop their books down the staircase. Happy people walk into lampposts and feel like dorks.

Happy people and unhappy people are all the same, except for this:

♦ Happy people have a sense of joy.
♦ Unhappy people lack that inner joy.

There are people who have won a million dollar lottery who are miserable. They divorced their spouses, wasted their money, and filed for bankruptcy. There are others who have cancer and yet they try to enjoy every day. They are grateful for little things like the company of the people they love.

Many of us believe the happy people are those who have everything going their way. They have large boats, huge houses, sports cars, and thin waists. Sometimes they are happy. But it's not because of the things they own. They choose to be happy. They rely on something inside them, rather than on possessions.

A Christian has an extra reason to enjoy life. We are given happiness—real joy—in our walk with God. We know we are trying to walk with God and that walk gives our lives even more meaning. Even Christians can be unhappy from time to time, but they never lose that inner joy.

> *"To the man who pleases him, God gives wisdom, knowledge and happiness."*
>
> *Ecclesiastes 2:26*

Keep thinking

1. Do you see yourself as a happy, upbeat person or as a bucket of mud?
2. Who do you know who has a tough life and yet seems happy?
3. Have you ever felt close to God? How did that make you feel?

A Clothes Nut

Katie never saw a sweater she didn't love. When she walked down the halls at school, her eyes bugged out every time she saw someone wearing a new outfit. And Katie was crazy about new sweatshirts—especially the brightly colored ones with neat imprints and clever designs. She envied every one she saw.

She wasn't exactly dressed in rags, but she didn't own any of the expensive stuff and her fashions maybe were not exactly on the cutting edge. She wanted desperately to own expensive clothes—to be on the cutting edge. So every day was a horror movie for Katie. In the morning she fussed and complained about her clothes. If her parents were around, Katie grumbled a little louder to make sure they heard how unhappy she was. When she finally got to school, Katie felt awful every time she saw a nice piece of clothing march past in the hallway.

An otherwise capable teenager ended up in the pits because she couldn't stop envying everybody else. Katie couldn't become thankful for what she had because she was too busy criticizing every speck of material in her closet or on her body. And she couldn't appreciate her parents because she considered them cheap and uncaring.

Envy has the power to make us unthankful and unappreciative. When we watch others and want what they have, we ask for trouble. We will always find someone who has better clothes, a better home, a better car. If we don't learn to be happy with what we have, every day will be like eating the spinach and liver special.

The apostle Paul said he had known what it was like to have plenty. Maybe Paul had a dozen pairs of sandals, fourteen tunics along with a cupboard full of bread and dried locusts—whatever it was they considered the good life.

But Paul said he also knew what it was like to be in want. Maybe he was out of shekels, low on honey, and had lost his last bowl of barley mix. He understood what it was like to be dead broke.

Whether he was doing well or whether he was scratching for his next meal, Paul learned to be content. He wasn't going to let his circumstances turn him into a bitter grouch.

That was part of what he had learned by living with God. Paul wasn't going to get confused by envying the turbans and tunics he saw other people wearing. God had given him the peace to appreciate everything he had.

> *"I am not saying this because I am in need, for I have learned to be content whatever the circumstances. I know what it is to be in need, and I know what it is to have plenty. I have learned the secret of being content in any and every situation, whether well fed or hungry, whether living in plenty or in want. I can do everything through him who gives me strength."*
> *Philippians 4:11-13*

Keep thinking

1. Do you thank your parents for your clothes?
2. Have you thanked God for the good things you own?

Just a "Little" Sex

Just a "little" sex, that's the big push. Not many people walk up and say, "How would you like to have sex?" Even in an open society where we see sex in movies, watch it on television, and read about it in books, the push is still the same, "Why don't we try a 'little' sex?"

A little sex sounds exciting, adventurous, like trying a little bit of danger, or a little bit of fear. A little sex must be like watching a horror movie: you expect a rush but you are sure no one will get hurt.

Let's be frank. You are old enough for frankness. By a little sex we are talking about a couple exploring each other with their hands. Someone, sometime, is going to try to convince you that there's nothing wrong with that. "Touching body parts never killed anybody" is what their argument will be. "It's not like we are going to do it," they will explain.

When that moment comes (and it might be years before it does), you will have some tough decisions to make. Do you want to play with fire and take a chance on getting seriously burned, or do you want to draw the line immediately? How you make that decision can affect you for years.

There are a lot of people who wanted to mess with something "a little" and ended up with big problems:

♦ A man with one eye who couldn't control a little BB.
♦ A friend with one leg who fooled with a little dynamite.
♦ A girl with severe burns who played with a little fire.

♦ A person without fingers on one hand because he messed a little with a buzz saw.

And I know a girl who is lonely and bitter today because she was talked into trying a little sex when she was a teenager.

Often it's the little things that get you. God knew that. That's why God told us to hold off on sex.

> "It is God's will that you should be holy; that you
> should avoid sexual immorality; that each of you
> should learn to control his [or her] own body."
> 1 Thessalonians 4:3-4

Keep thinking

1. Is there pressure for you and others your age to have sex?
2. What are some good ways to avoid sex at your age?

Who Is Number One?

When I was a child, my family lived in a rented home in downtown Washington, D.C. Once a month the landlord and his wife walked through the neighborhood, stopping at each door to collect the rent.

We stood in awe of this mysterious couple who owned the house we lived in. Where did they come from and to where did they return after they took our money? How did they come to own these buildings? What were they like in the house they lived in—wherever that was?

That was our introduction to the word *lord.* The landlord was someone who owned and controlled the land. He had power and money. If we angered him, the landlord could demand that we move out almost immediately.

Later when I thought of Jesus Christ as Lord, naturally I compared him with my old landlord. Did that mean Jesus was some mysterious person who came silently into my life once a month and who could throw us out at any moment?

The title Lord confused and frightened me. I thought Jesus was the grouchy landlord in the sky.

After some time I learned a new use of the term Lord. Lord is someone who is in charge. When I let Jesus become my Lord, I allowed the Son of God to take charge of my life.

He influences:
♦ How I feel.
♦ How I treat others.
♦ How I handle money.

- ♦ How I process anger.
- ♦ My attitudes.
- ♦ My value system.
- ♦ How I serve others.

Christ would like to take charge of everything I do, but most of the time I am not willing to let him run the entire ship. Some days Jesus is in charge of more than he is other days.

Today I have asked Christ to control my temper, but I want to handle my own finances. Like most of us, I find it hard to be consistent.

The most important step is to accept the Son of God as number one in our lives. When we acknowledge that Jesus should be in charge, we start to let him call the shots. And Jesus is happy to accept the job.

"But in your hearts set apart Christ as Lord."
1 Peter 3:15

Keep thinking

1. Have you ever felt afraid to let Christ be in charge? Do you know why you are afraid?
2. Can you think of an area of your life where you would like for Jesus Christ to take control and help you?

Growing Up Fast

Let's get on with it. Nobody wants to grow up slowly. Who wants to be a child forever? Worse yet, who wants to be treated like a kid by parents, teachers, or the clerk at the grocery store.

What's the fastest way to grow up and be respected by most people? There is a formula: Try to be more like Jesus. If you work at living a Christian life, some things will happen:

♦ You will try not to hurt people.
♦ You will say fewer ugly things about others.
♦ You will try to tell the truth.
♦ You will try to keep your promises.
♦ You will refuse to steal.
♦ You will try to control your anger.
♦ You will try not to get even.
♦ You will respect the law.
♦ You will help others.
♦ You will refuse to pick fights.
♦ You will share what you have.

The list could go on, but you get the idea. No one is grown-up because of his or her size. Some very large people do childish things. Being a grown-up means acting grown-up. If you throw tantrums, suck your thumb, and toss your plate on the floor, you are acting like a child and should be treated like a 3-year-old.

People aren't grown-up because they say they are grown-up. If you say you are a bird, you still can't fly. You can announce that you are a coconut tree, but the hard part is producing the coconuts.

Everyone wants to be grown-up. We want to be mature and treated like adults. That usually happens to people who act like adults.

Don't ask how broad your shoulders are or how many pounds you can lift. Neither drugs nor alcohol nor tobacco ever made a boy into a man or a girl into a woman. Being grown-up has to do with our behavior.

Jesus can do a great many things for us. One of the most important is to change the way we act.

Become a follower and a believer in Jesus as the Son of God and watch how that decision changes your behavior. You might even be surprised how fast you grow up.

> *"Instead, speaking the truth in love, we will in all things grow up into him who is the Head, that is, Christ."*
>
> *Ephesians 4:15*

Keep thinking

1. Are you a believer and follower of Jesus? Explain what that means to you.
2. How does believing in Jesus affect your behavior?

Wallflowers

Each of us has to make a choice. Do we want to mix with others, get to know people, and enjoy life, or do we want to withdraw, be lonely, and act afraid?

The choice isn't easy. Mixing with others at church and school can be hard. It involves taking risks. Some people will accept us while others may treat us like leftover cardboard.

But the risk is worth it. Only by taking chances do we find friends. Only by becoming involved do we discover people who care for us.

Millions of teens are scared to death when it comes to meeting people. They are wallflowers. They stand close to the wall, making sure they don't get hurt. They imagine that no one will notice them hiding in the shadows. They are shy to the max.

The biggest problem with shyness is that it hurts. Most everybody wants to meet people. They want to have a good time. They want to express opinions. But some people are so afraid to give it a try that they slide back and hide beside the wall.

Some people seem naturally outgoing. They jump into any group and talk like politicians. On the other hand, 80 percent of us report feeling painfully shy at some time in our lives.

The Bible tells us that God wants to pull us away from the wall. God wants us to shake loose and get out into the mainstream. God isn't happy to see us hiding in the shadows too scared to say hello to anyone.

If we have a timid spirit, God did not give it to us. God wants us to take a chance and get involved with people.

We can pray for confidence and count on God to back us up.

Being a wallflower is one choice. Mixing with friends is a better one.

"For God did not give us a spirit of timidity, but a spirit of power, of love and of self-discipline."
2 Timothy 1:7

Keep thinking

1. Do you find it hard to mix with friends?
2. What could you do to overcome shyness?

The Battle over Booze

The people who keep statistics tell us that during junior high or middle school almost 90 percent of the students will try alcohol. A few sixth graders taste booze, and for seventh graders the figures begin to skyrocket.

For most of those young people drinking sounds exciting. They believe they are entering the adult world and alcohol is a sign of how grown-up they have become. After all, they argue, they are ready to handle anything.

But "anything" includes kids around them who have become messed up with booze—young people who are in trouble with the law or who are flunking out of school because they can't leave the bottle alone. Later on some of these teens can't manage college or tech school because they depend on a few drinks to get them through the evening or even through the day. Then there are those who have died from drinking and driving.

Despite all this, many teens don't want to miss out on what might be a good time. They don't want to be left out from a party or a few laughs or a screeching ride in a car.

Let's face it—you and your friends are bright kids. You are aware of the harm alcohol could do. There is little to gain by dragging out all of the horror stories again, even though those stories are true.

But why be in such a hurry to try everything? You might think you simply can't wait. The word wait may seem to grab you by the throat. It's hard, but sometimes the smartest thing a person can do is to hold off before trying something.

Drinking alcohol is a serious, sometimes life-changing, decision. It makes sense to wait before you cross that very adult bridge.

The decision is up to each person. No one can make it for you. There is plenty of booze available if you are determined to get it. But before you decide, consider this: A lot of people who really have it together wait and make the alcohol decision when they are older.

> *"Do not get drunk on wine, which leads to de-bauchery. Instead, be filled with the Spirit."*
> *Ephesians 5:18*

Keep thinking

1. How much damage do you see alcohol has caused in others' lives?
2. Why do you or your friends want to drink?
3. What would happen if you waited to make a decision about alcohol until you are 21?

Those Magazines

There are plenty of magazines available with pictures of naked people. I'm not talking about *National Geographic*. I'm talking about "those magazines." Some have colorful photos of women, some of men, and some of both. Maybe someone has brought a copy to school. Maybe someone's parents have copies and you've seen those. Maybe you noticed them behind the counter at the convenience store and wondered—just a little—what it would be like to look at one.

If you were to look at one, chances are the ceiling won't collapse on you, your hair won't fall out, and God is not likely to give you a heart attack. Matter of fact, since the magazines are so common, most young people will see them sooner or later and live to tell of it.

These kinds of magazines probably are not going to go away, so we ought to ask a few serious questions about them. What does happen if you check out the beautiful nude bodies?

Question 1: Will the magazines become an obsession? Perhaps. No one plans it that way, but some people become addicted to gazing at nude bodies. These people have no social life, they aren't interested in school, and they have few other activities. It becomes easy to withdraw and "live" with pornographic magazines.

Question 2: Will the magazines cause you to look at people as mere objects? There's a good chance. Many people look at males and females only as bodies. They are something to be used and discarded. If you grow up

51

thinking that way, you might also look at boyfriends, girl-friends, husbands, and wives as sex objects to be used.

Often a nude person in a magazine ceases to be a person. We don't know anything about the person's personality, family, hopes, or fears. If we spend too much time poring over magazines, we might begin to see others as people without feelings.

Question 3: Will the magazines begin to draw you away from God? Probably. One reason some people read these magazines is because they are forbidden. It's exciting to "sneak a peek." But with the excitement comes guilt. Some feel so guilty that they drift far from God. As a result they are miserable, lonely, and isolated.

They didn't expect it to happen, but a steady diet of nude pictures has made them feel dirty and cheap. When we are down on ourselves, we frequently feel separated from God. Our fellowship or closeness seems weak.

The world of skin isn't going to go away. Skimpy bathing suits, nude statues, and erotic movies are all around us. The important thing is that we control ourselves so that lust does not become the greatest force in our lives.

> *"That each of you should learn to control his own body in a way that is holy and honorable, not in passionate lust like the heathen."*
> *1 Thessalonians 4:4*

Keep thinking

1. Are magazines of nude men and women available in your area? Where?
2. What is the biggest problem with them as far as you are concerned?

Just Say Yes!

Every day after school Brenda walks part way home with her friend, Terri. Usually they talk about teachers, boys, or clothes, and they laugh and worry together. When they come to Lincoln Boulevard, they sign off and go in separate directions.

As Brenda walks the last four blocks by herself, she is a different person. Inside her mind, Brenda imagines that she is on the school council, giving an impassioned plea for lower lunch prices. A block later, she pictures herself with a part in the school play. Brenda imagines herself dramatically repeating a line and hearing the audience roar with laughter at her comedy talent.

Finally reaching her house, the teenager bounds up the stairs and scurries indoors. Like so many of us, Brenda knows that inside her quiet frame there is a fascinating, capable person. But she is afraid to open up and become who she really is.

There are opportunities all around her. Classes, clubs, groups, and volunteer organizations practically beg Brenda to untie herself and become part of them. But this reluctant teenager can't bring herself to say yes. The uncertainty, the fear, the apprehension of the unknown are always too much for Brenda.

The shame of it all is that God has given Brenda a box that holds lots of gifts and talents. Brenda may know she has the box, but she is afraid to open it. She is too tied up to pull back the top and see what God has for her.

Imagine if your parent gives you a birthday present and you neglect to open it. You admire the package and are grateful for the thoughtfulness, but you are too shy to see what is in the box. You'd be acting just like Brenda.

The best way to open the present God has given each of us is to say yes. You must decide to swallow your fear and give life a shot. Only by trying can you discover what you can do and what interests you.

For four blocks Brenda lives out what she would like to do. For four blocks she stretches her talent and dreams of what she could become. If she would say yes to more opportunities, Brenda could live out her gifts every day.

> *"We have different gifts, according to the grace given us. If a man's gift is prophesying, let him use it in proportion to his faith. If it is serving, let him serve; if it is teaching, let him teach; if it is encouraging, let him encourage; if it is contributing to the needs of others, let him give generously; if it is leadership, let him govern diligently; if it is showing mercy, let him do it cheerfully."*
>
> *Romans 12:6-8*

Keep thinking

1. What would you like to try?
2. What's keeping you from trying it?

Stepparents

Remember the story of Cinderella and her wicked step-mother? She also had a couple of pretty lousy stepsisters who made mice want to run and hide. I think stories like that give steprelatives a bad rap. There may be some mean stepparents around, but most of them are kind and loving people.

With so many divorces and some deaths of parents, more and more teens are growing up with stepparents in the family. Often two stepparents are inherited, one married to each parent.

I remember getting a stepmother when I was a teen. It felt different having another woman enter my life. At first it was hard to figure out what the relationship was. Was she really a mother? Was I really a son?

We got along very well. What helped the most was to see how much my stepmother meant to my dad. To know that she played such an important role in his life made me appreciate how good she was for everybody.

That wasn't the way I would have planned my family. We all wanted the neat little package: a mother, a father, three children, a dog, and a microwave oven. But usually life doesn't come like frozen dinners. Things go wrong and sometimes we get kicked in the head.

If you have a stepparent, there are a few things you might try to make it a good relationship.

1. *Try to thank God for your stepparent.* Accepting a stepparent with a good attitude can help make the two of you friends.

2. *You take the first big step.* Don't sit back and wait to see how the other person is going to act. Make your stepparents feel like a million bucks and it will be easier for him or her to feel relaxed with you.

3. *Make it a point to talk.* If this person is new to you, great communication is all the more important. Even when it feels awkward, sit down and start a conversation.

4. *Don't expect your stepparent to be perfect.* Even the best of parents suffer from goofiness some days.

5. *Pray for your stepparent.* Ask God to give him or her a good night's sleep, rich coffee beans, an excellent day at the office, and nice weather—whatever it takes to make his or her day go well. It's hard to stay grouchy with someone you are praying for.

The most famous stepchild in the world was Jesus Christ. An angel told Joseph to accept Jesus, even though he had no earthly father. Joseph wasn't sure how well this would work out, but Joseph finally agreed.

God had only one Son and God trusted that child with a stepfather. Joseph protected Jesus, provided for him, and furnished a happy home.

> *"When Joseph woke up, he did what the angel of the Lord had commanded him and took Mary home as his wife. But he had no union with her until she gave birth to a son. And he gave him the name Jesus."*
>
> Matthew 1:24-25

Keep thinking

1. Who do you know who has a good stepparent?
2. What makes that relationship work so well?

A Hurry to Grow Up

When 16-year-old Matthew invited her to go along, 13-year-old Nina was flattered. She loved hanging out with older kids, and the chance to cruise around in a beat-up Chevy was a thrill she couldn't turn down. Most of the time the car had three or four of Matthew's high school friends leaning out the windows. Usually the girls shouted crude remarks at bystanders as the old Chevy spun out or cut corners too close.

This was Nina's idea of fun—to get in with the grown-up crowd, to find a faster lane, to find some genuine excitement. On the weekends Matthew would usually find a party and the entire carload would invade that home or apartment. Inside there would be plenty of boys, a large supply of alcohol, and sometimes marijuana.

The alcohol made her light-headed, loud, and goofy. The boys were close, pushy, and physical. Because the parties ended late, Nina usually got into trouble with her parents.

Fortunately Nina never got into any serious trouble. Except for hassles with her parents, the young teen didn't have any brushes with the law, she didn't get really drunk, and she kept the boys under reasonable control. But one late night, after an ugly confrontation with her father, Nina sat alone in her room and thought it over.

Did she really want to move this fast? Did she want to make hard, tough choices this early in life? Did she even understand what was happening to her mind and body? She decided it wasn't really any fun playing in deep water if she had to always stand on her toes to keep from drowning.

The next day Nina found Matthew at the drive-in and told her friend the truth.

"I really like you," Nina said. "You're a blast to be with. But the car and the parties are too fast for me. I need to go back and hang out with my own age group. Hey, but I'll look for you when I stop in at the drive-in."

Nina decided to enjoy being a young teenager for a few years before she became an older teenager.

> *"Be happy, young man, while you are young,*
> *and let your heart give you joy in the days of*
> *your youth."*
>
> *Ecclesiastes 11:9*

Keep thinking

1. Do you ever feel like you have too many choices to make too quickly?
2. Have you ever refused to do something because you felt you weren't ready?

Walking Dates

When you walk through the local mall you can see them. They stop at a store window and talk about the new clothes hanging there. Later you see the same pair sipping cola in the fast-food restaurant.

They look like good people. Each is in his or her early teens. Too young to drive, they are on a walking date. Later they may pop in to see a movie and each will pay his or her way.

Sometimes they drift around the halls with two or three other couples, laughing nervously. It looks like fun as they get to know each other on a Saturday evening.

There's nothing wrong with a walking date, but it isn't for everybody. A great many teenagers think they are better off hanging out with groups of friends and keeping everything light. They know there is plenty of time to get to know someone on a one-to-one basis later. They don't want to get involved too early.

There was an attractive girl named Angie who never had a date until she was in college. The boys she wanted to go out with never seemed to notice her, and she never got up the courage to ask them out.

But one day in college, young men started calling her for dates, and she felt comfortable asking out guys too. The fact that she had dated no one before college made no difference in the long run. Angie was patient and Angie was glad.

Young people who feel they have to get hooked up as soon as possible are sometimes asking for a lot of pain.

Those who stay calm and wait it out are frequently grateful that they didn't let their lives get too complicated too early.

"Boyfriends are nice, but they are also the pits," Vickie said when she was in the ninth grade.

Walking dates and riding dates have much to offer. But they are also demanding and sometimes frustrating.

Patience usually pays off. Young people who are in a huge hurry to get matched up often find it a terrible drain.

"The end of a matter is better than its beginning, and patience is better than pride."

Ecclesiates 7:8

Keep thinking

1. When do you think teens should start dating?
2. How would your life be affected if you never dated as a teenager?

Hanging in There

"Am I going to go to school all of my life?"

Do you know someone who has become disgusted with school? Have you ever felt that you are going to be in school forever? Most young people become tempted sometime to quit and get a job. In some places a huge number of teens give up on school each year.

A survey in San Antonio, Texas, found that among some student groups almost half drop out before graduating from high school. Half of those had quit before finishing the ninth grade. That means if there were 30 students in a class, 7 would not finish junior high or middle school. Of those 30, 15 never would complete high school.

When students drop out, their life choices become tremendously limited. Most employers don't want them. Their ability to make a living is seriously hindered. Life is terribly tough for people who don't hang in there.

The pressure to quit can become terribly heavy. Maybe your grades start dragging and one of the teachers gets on your case. Maybe your parents get too pushy, or you feel you don't have enough money to spend. Life as a teen can get mean.

But inside you know that the people who hang in there usually get the most out of life. You know that life without an education can be a ride on misery mountain.

When the pressure gets rough, it pays to stick close to Jesus. Jesus is able to encourage us when we want to toss in the towel. He often reminds us of important strengths like courage, hope, and perseverance. If we are willing to stick it out through school, Jesus is willing to hang in there with us.

The apostle Paul must have thought often about giving up. Life as a follower of Jesus was hard back then. But Paul was able to pull himself together and say, "I press on toward the goal to win the prize for which God has called me heavenward in Christ Jesus" (Phil. 3:14).

Pressing on—that's how Paul saw it. Pulling out is seldom the answer to anything.

Hang in there and God will hang in there with you.

"Consider it pure joy, my brothers, whenever you face trials of many kinds, because you know that testing of your faith develops perseverance. Perseverance must finish its work so that you may be mature and complete, not lacking anything."

James 1:2-4

Keep thinking

1. What are some reasons why you or your friends want to quit school?
2. Have you ever asked Jesus to help you make it all the way through school?

Feeling Rotten

Everybody gave Eric a hard time. The clothes he wore were a little different, the religion his family followed wasn't popular, and his sense of humor seemed strange. Most of his classmates thought of Eric as a nerd. They called him names, picked him last when choosing teams, and made him the brunt of lots of jokes.

One of the people who teased Eric was an eighth grader named Lance. Usually Lance never gave it much thought. He simply jumped in and did what everyone else did. Everyone enjoyed making Eric's life miserable.

During lunch one day Lance sat at the end of a long table and watched as two kids made fun of Eric. As they needled Eric he tried to laugh as he normally did, but Lance could see the pain on the teen's face.

For some mysterious reason Lance felt sick over what he saw. And something in his conscience bothered him. For the first time Lance realized that he was one of the bad guys and that what he did was cruel. At that moment Lance felt rotten.

Since Lance went to church regularly, he did something he almost never did. He bowed his head at the table and told God he was sorry. No big scene. He didn't cry, fall on his knees, or tear his shirt. Lance told God how he honestly felt. He was sorry.

Then, without making a scene, Lance stood up, picked up his tray, and went over and sat next to Eric. He didn't apologize to Eric, though he wanted to. Instead Lance simply sat down and began to talk to him about nothing in particular.

Sometimes it hits us like a brick. We have been treating someone like garbage. When it hits us, we suddenly have this rotten feeling. That's good. A rotten feeling will often cause us to do something about it.

When we feel terrible over something we have done, a good place to go first is to God. We ask God to forgive us. Because of Jesus, God forgives us right away. Then we go to the person we mistreated and we straighten out the situation.

If we take care of those two things, the rotten feeling should go away.

"If we confess our sins, he is faithful and just and will forgive us our sins and purify us from all unrighteousness."

1 John 1:9

Keep thinking

1. Are you presently treating someone terribly?
2. Would you like to treat that person differently?
3. Wouldn't this be a good day to start treating him or her better?

When you Don't Feel Normal

Which one of these describes how you feel?
- ◆ Do you ever feel like you have an embarrassing laugh?
- ◆ Do you feel left out of the really important things?
- ◆ Do you feel like your appearance is different?
- ◆ Are you afraid to speak up because others might make fun of you?
- ◆ Are you afraid to give your opinion?
- ◆ Are you afraid to try new things because you might fail?

If any or all of these are true of you, there is good news. You are perfectly normal. These feelings bother almost all of us. They bother athletes, kings, presidents, movie stars, geniuses, and tightrope walkers. If some of these problems drive you half crazy, you aren't abnormal, you aren't subnormal, you are just like the rest of the human race.

We look at others and think, "She must be cool. She has it all together. I wish I could be like her." But if you get to know her, you find out she has all of the exact feelings that you have.

You aren't abnormal. We are all related to each other. Most of us sit home hoping someone will call us. We want to get together with our friends, but we are afraid they will turn us down. Almost everybody feels that way.

Most of us feel like we look funny.
- ◆ How often have you said you have the worst hair in the world?

- ♦ How often have you said your clothes look terrible?
- ♦ How often have you felt embarrassed to wear your old coat?
- ♦ How often have you worried what to say if you were to be alone with that special person?

Welcome to the club. Almost all of us feel that way. Disc jockeys, musicians, football players, models, and sword swallowers all feel the same. You are as normal as a snowflake in Buffalo.

What really gets us messed up is the feeling that we want to be better than everyone else. We want the best hair, the best singing voice, the best clothes, the best house.

Be happy to be normal. That's what most of us are. It's the feeling that we have to beat everyone at everything that gets our minds twisted around.

We are normal and we should be thankful that we are.

"Do not think of yourself more highly than you ought."

Romans 12:3

Keep thinking

1. What are you thankful for about yourself?
2. What do you consider normal about yourself?
3. Do you feel a need to compete with others?

Sex Isn't What You Think

"I was scared to death," Brad explained. "There we were in the car, trying to have sex as fast as we could, and it wasn't any fun at all. I'm not sure it was worth all that."

Millions of teens could say something like this. Sex holds out a great promise of enjoyment and excitement, but under the wrong conditions it's nothing but a big hassle. People can get hurt, lives can be affected, entire families can be embarrassed.

Many young people refuse to believe this, but if sex is going to be satisfying it belongs in a marriage.

♦ Safe sex is married sex.
♦ Caring sex is married sex.
♦ Healthy sex is married sex.
♦ Esteem-building sex is married sex.
♦ Guilt-free sex is married sex.
♦ Faithful sex is married sex.

It doesn't do much good to try to frighten teenagers. Most young people think they are scare-proof. Instead, let's just look at a few simple facts.

Fact 1: Of the young people who are sexually active, one in four contracts a disease from sex.

Fact 2: You may think you won't get pregnant, but one million teenage girls will this year.

Fact 3: A huge number of teenagers (especially girls) do not enjoy sex because the act is so risky, confusing, and empty.

Why does God warn us against having sex outside of marriage? Is God just that great hall monitor in the sky who likes to boss people around? Or does God care about teens and hate to see them get hurt?

God is a loving parent. God isn't mean, grumpy, or moody. God doesn't shout just for the fun of it.

As a loving parent, God puts his arm around your shoulders and says, "Sex isn't what you think. Save it for marriage and you can get the most out of it. I'd really hate to see you get hurt."

Thank you, Heavenly Father, for telling us the facts of life.

> *"Flee from sexual immorality. All other sins a man commits are outside his body, but he who sins sexually sins against his own body."*
> *1 Corinthians 6:18*

Keep thinking

1. Why do you think kids are in such a hurry to try sex?
2. Is the need for sex mostly physical or a need to be wanted, or just thrill-seeking?
3. What are two good reasons why you should wait?

Close to Your Parents

When you become a teenager, it sometimes means you and your parents begin to drift apart. There is a great deal of stress on independence and discovering who you are and all of those new things. As your life gets reshuffled, it's easy to lose close contact with your parents. Loss of close contact can make you feel lonely and sometimes discouraged.

But as a fast-moving teenager, how can you keep in close touch with your parents without feeling like a little kid? It takes some extra work, but your relationship is worth the effort.

The goal is to strive for open communication between you and your parents. To get close without being smothered, try this: Make a short list of what your parents have experienced as they grew up:

♦ How did they feel about the Vietnam War?
♦ Did your mother ever wear a mini-skirt?
♦ Did they go to church as children? What was it like?
♦ What was their junior high school like?
♦ What were their brothers or sisters like back then?
♦ Did they have jobs after school?
♦ Did they ride a school bus (or a covered wagon)?
♦ What was their favorite music in junior high?
♦ What did they think of Elvis?
♦ How did your parents meet?
♦ How long did your parents date?
♦ What were some of their happiest moments to- gether?

- ◆ What did your grandparents do that was fun as a family?
- ◆ What were their favorite sayings to your mother or father?
- ◆ Did your parents and grandparents play together, work together, and worship together?
- ◆ Did they travel?

Too many teenagers see their parents as strangers. They don't know how their mother and father became who they are today. Usually if you show an interest in your parents as people, the family can pull closer together because you will better understand each other.

Parents will open up if they think their children care about them. Stay close. Keep conversation going. Ask your parents how it was and how it is in their lives.

> *"When I was a boy in my father's house, still tender, and an only child of my mother, he taught me and said, 'Lay hold of my words with all your heart; keep my commands and you will live.'"*
>
> Proverbs 4:3-4

Keep thinking

1. What would you like to know about your parents?
2. When would be a good time to ask some of these questions?
3. The next time you write a paper for school, consider writing about your mother, father, or a stepparent.

Kicking Trash Cans

When Kyle became angry at his brother, he stomped up to his bedroom, swung his foot back, and kicked the San Francisco 49ers trash can across the floor. When it finally rolled to a stop, Kyle could see the deep dent he had planted in the middle of the can.

We all understand what Kyle did. It's easy to get angry once in a while, and sometimes we take it out on the furniture. But what if Kyle went to his room every night and kicked the trash can or hit the wall or punched the door? If Kyle has to kick, hit, or punch something regularly, he might have a serious problem. When a person has a pattern of violent behavior, he or she ought to be concerned about what is going on.

Suppose Gina exaggerated when she told stories about herself. If she said, "No one is ever nice to me" or "There were 12 girls who wanted to use my new tape recorder" when there were only two, you might start to wonder why Gina has to stretch every story she tells about herself.

We all know how to exaggerate. But what if we have a pattern of almost always stretching the truth? Maybe that is a sign that we have a problem.

The Bible teaches us that we all make mistakes. We commit errors; we sin. But some people have gone off the deep end and are in a pattern of doing something wrong day in and day out.

Watch out for patterns:

- ◆ Are you out to fool people most of the time?
- ◆ Do you look for ways to cheat your friends?

- ◆ Is lying your daily way of talking?
- ◆ Are you busy trying to get even with others?
- ◆ Are you always trying to trash your brother or sister?
- ◆ Are you greedy and do you try to keep everything for yourself?

It's wrong to lie once or cheat once, but people who do them regularly are falling into an evil routine. They need to check themselves before they develop a habit they can't break later.

Sometimes teens are accused of not knowing how to tell the truth because they lie for so long they don't know the difference.

All of us do goofy things, but what you need to worry about the most is the patterns you develop. If you do something often enough, you may not be able to see what's wrong with it.

> *"Do not conform any longer to the pattern of this world, but be transformed by the renewing of your mind."*
>
> *Romans 12:2*

Keep thinking

1. What bad habit or pattern have you developed?
2. Are you concerned enough to break the pattern now?
3. Would you like to ask God to help you control the situation?

You Can Teach English

You can teach English? Sounds like a crazy idea, doesn't it? Here you are, barely able to identify an adjective and slightly confused over prepositions, and someone suggests you teach English. You can't tell a simile from a diphthong or a metaphor from a matador. Teaching English might seem goofy.

But it isn't so weird. Schools are discovering that the best way to learn is to teach. If you explain a limerick to a friend, you are far more likely to remember what a limerick is. On the other hand, if you sit in a room alone and try to memorize that a limerick is a humorous rhyming verse of five lines, you could go bonkers.

All over the country thousands of teens are teaching subjects to their friends. By teaching friends, young tutors are learning about limericks, metaphors, prepositions, and even matadors.

They meet with their friend or friends during study hall or at lunch or at home or at the pizza parlor. When they describe a subject to someone else, that subject is more likely to lock into their brain.

College students have done this for years. They often meet in groups to study a subject and everyone seems to learn better.

When you explain a subject to another person, that subject is far more likely to become part of you.

What subject or class are you having trouble with? Find a friend who is also having difficulty in the same area. Share what you know with that person, and let that person share with you what he or she knows. This can be done with some of the hardest material.

In the early church, Christians developed a similar pattern. When men and women believed in Jesus Christ and learned more about the Son of God, they turned around and taught someone else. By teaching others both spread the gospel and learned more for themselves.

It doesn't pay to sit and be confused all alone. Find some friends, share what you know about physics, math, history, English, or even darts. We all learn better by sharing with others.

> *"Teach these great truths to trustworthy men who will, in turn, pass them on to others."*
> *2 Timothy 2:2 (TLB)*

Keep thinking

1. What subject would you like help with?
2. Who could you get together with and teach each other?
3. When are you going to do that?

Unfair Teachers

On the first day of school Mike made a wisecrack in shop class and Mr. McCann chewed him out. No one thought it was a big deal. Mike managed to keep his comments to himself after that. He wasn't looking for trouble.

Unfortunately Mr. McCann never got over the incident. From that day on the teacher refused to back off. He spoke gruffly to the student and he was terribly critical of whatever Mike did.

The mistreatment was so obvious that the entire class felt sorry for Mike. The teen was a smart person who knew he couldn't change Mr. McCann, so he made a few mature decisions:

1. Mike promised himself he wouldn't do anything to further aggravate the man. Since his teacher held a great deal of power, Mike refused to go to war with him and make things worse. Smart people know when to back off.

2. He decided to be kind. Mike always said hello, smiled, and went about his work in a businesslike fashion.

3. Mike made a calendar and counted off how many days he had left in the class. This way he knew the pressure would not last forever.

4. He picked out one person and talked to that person about his situation when he had to. Mike didn't make the situation worse by complaining every day to everyone about what a grouch Mr. McCann was.

Instead of flying off and hurting himself and his future, Mike took a mature approach. He reasoned the situation out, took control of himself, and tried to minimize the damage.

Another student, Tony, faced the same mean teacher and began to irritate Mr. McCann. After a month of yelling at each other, Tony dropped the class and spent an extra semester in high school.

Most teachers are responsible professionals. But a few teachers are miserable toads. Every teenager knows that. The students who go to war in a battle they can't win usually end up getting hurt.

If possible, make every attempt to get along with a bone-headed teacher. When it's not possible, head for the school counselor's office. Whatever you do, don't hurt your future by blowing up and trying to get even.

> *"My dear brothers, take note of this: Everyone should be quick to listen, slow to speak and slow to become angry, for man's anger does not bring about the righteous life that God de-sires."*
>
> *James 1:19-20*

Keep thinking

1. How do you handle a grouchy teacher?
2. When would you go to a school counselor to discuss an unfair teacher?

Settling Arguments

The schools in San Francisco are trying a new approach to handling arguments among students. They have set aside a special conflict room. If two or more students are angry about something, they can go to this designated room and have someone help settle their differences.

Whoever is arguing can choose whether they want two teenagers or an adult to help them with their problem. The people they meet with have had 16 hours of training in how to settle arguments.

Many teenagers need a way to blow off steam and to express their frustration and anger without resorting to violence. Instead of picking up a brick, throwing a punch or—as some severely distraught teens have done—going home and looking for a parent's gun, they can simply head for the conflict room and tell someone what the deal is. The helpers in the room listen calmly, sort out what is at the heart of the problem, and suggest ways to resolve the conflict.

Serious conflicts may not happen as often in your school, but facts have shown that many teenagers don't know how to get along. A young person in Washington, D.C., was walking down the hall when he waved to a student he knew fairly well. The student he waved to merely shrugged his shoulders but didn't wave back.

The person who waved became so angry at the apparent snub that he waited for the student after school. After a few ugly words the two teenagers slugged it out in a terrible fight. They both got hurt, and they both got suspended from school.

Many of us get frustrated when things don't go our way. We often feel put down and put off. We aren't treated fairly, get left out, and sometimes we are absolutely abused. This makes us want to blow up and lash out.

When we attack, the situation usually gets worse. But most of the time we don't know what else to do.

Having a system to settle arguments might be a big help. Maybe that is something you could suggest to the student council or to the principal.

God doesn't want us thrashing it out like a frenzied shark slashing and tearing away at its victim. God wants us to settle disputes and quarrels in a calm, sensible way. Our God would like to see us live in peace, not in battle.

If we ask God for wisdom, we may be shown some good ways to resolve our anger. Hitting people doesn't do much good for anyone.

> *"A hot-tempered man stirs up dissension,*
> *but a patient man calms a quarrel."*
> *Proverbs 15:18*

Keep thinking

1. How would a program like the one in San Francisco work in your school?
2. When you are extremely angry, what do you do to calm down?

A Discombobulated Bus

Do you ride the school bus? If you do, have you noticed how many students doze off with their heads bobbing down on their chests? Do you see kids with their heads tossed back, mouths wide open as the bus bounces along?

A few students are probably hurrying through their history books before they get to class, trying to find out who won the Civil War. All kinds of young people, some with breakfast in hand, spread across the bus trying to cope in the early morning.

For some teenagers a bus ride is the perfect time to close their eyes and talk with God. Don't worry, no one will miss you. They'll think you have crashed back to slumberland or are trying to remember who was president after Kennedy.

In just a few quiet minutes, in the middle of a discombobulated bus, you could tell God how things are going. With a simple four or five sentences you can talk to God about your hopes, your fears, your worries, and the person you have a crush on. It's a great way to lay a few burdens down before the day gets carried away.

You might say, "Hey, God! You're great! I love having you around!" Ask God to help you be a little more loving to those you meet. Explain how you want to cut down the harshness and increase the kindness.

No need to make it a big deal. You don't have to impress God with long words, fancy names, or lots of thee's and thou's. God understands straightforward, honest, sincere talk. God appreciates a compliment, likes to hear how things are going, and enjoys helping out. God plays several roles, and one of them is friend. Talk to this heavenly friend as if you were at a lunchroom table, only not quite so loud.

Maybe buses aren't your thing. Try praying while riding in a car, doing your paper route (with your eyes open), running laps, or taking a shower—anyplace where your mind can take a few minutes out.

Tell God how it's going and how you would like it to go. Ask God if there is something that God wants you to do.

You and God are friends talking about the day. The big difference is you have a friend who can do anything.

"Pray continually."

1 Thessalonians 5:17

Keep thinking

1. When and where is a good time for you to talk to God?
2. What do you talk to God about the most?

It's Crazy Body Time

Have you ever noticed a class of 13-year-olds standing in line for lunch? A few are taller than the teachers and one or two look like they haven't grown since third grade. And it isn't just height. Some have arms that have stretched out of their sweaters; others can't find jeans to fit. A couple of the boys don't appear to have a muscle in their bodies.

It's crazy body time. I remember looking in a mirror when I was 13 and thinking I had trash can lids for ears. Day and night I worried about it, asked my friends how my ears looked, and tried to comb my hair over them. For a few weeks my ears were the biggest problem in my life.

Fortunately my fears about my ears were wiped away by one girl in her early 20s. I asked her about my ears and she said, with a warm smile, "You look fine." Then I started to worry about my feet.

Boys are likely to worry about their height when they hit the teen years. All boys want to be tall. When they see many of the girls taller than they are, it drives them nuts, especially at dances. They don't have much to be concerned over. Boys usually spurt up once or twice and often end up tall enough. A few boys don't reach their full height until they are out of high school.

Most of us learn to become happy with ourselves no matter how tall we get. We find out that character, kindness, and friendship are more important than size. But while you are growing like corn plants in July, it's hard to believe that size doesn't count.

If boys worry about height and ears, girls think every other day about breast size. We may call breasts other names, but no matter what we call them, breasts are one of the great interests among Americans. Other nationalities talk about them far less.

A 13- or 14-year-old girl might have little development or a great deal. Naturally she worries about growing too large or not growing at all. No matter how she grows, the girl is probably going to be teased. That teasing often comes from other girls as well as boys.

It's hard to be patient and accepting, but it is the best route. In your early teens there is no way of knowing how your body will turn out. The best attitude is to stay healthy, exercise, eat right, and let your body grow at its own pace.

Most of us will be happy with the finished product. God has designed a great machine that builds as we grow. It will be intriguing to see how wonderfully your body develops.

If you have specific questions about your growth, ask your parents, doctors, teachers, or possibly your youth counselors. When you know what is going on, you have little to fear as your body stretches out.

> *"I praise you because I am fearfully and wonderfully made; your works are wonderful, I know that full well."*
>
> *Psalms 139:14*

Keep thinking

1. List five good features about yourself.
2. When was the last time you thanked God for your body and health and growth?

What's Your Problem?

Beth was born with a special problem. Her doctors said Beth would never walk because of a bone defect.

Not only could she not walk, but years later both of her feet were removed and artificial limbs were added below her knees. Despite these serious problems, Beth went on to become a high school cheerleader at age 14.

Beth and her parents give God the credit for helping her overcome her awesome "problems."

All of us have problems. We have learning disabilities or weight problems. We are short or tall or have big feet. Some of us are sick. A few of us have seen the doctor so often we think he or she is a relative.

Sometimes it helps to know that other people have problems and they learned to work with them. Then we might not feel so alone and we might not think our situation is hopeless.

It's great to hear about young men with twisted feet who go on to become famous football kickers. Or to hear a captivating and energetic speaker who was terribly shy when she was in school. Or a good mother who came from parents who abused her. Recently a man told me how spending 30 days in jail turned his life around.

Everybody has a problem. You can see some people's problems right away. Others store up their problems inside and try to keep them hidden. But everybody has it tough somehow.

When you think about your own personal problems, it might help to remind yourself of this: God is not done working with you yet. God may show you ways to turn the problem into something good. God might make someone who can't see into a writer. Someone who has a speech impairment might become a speech teacher. Maybe God will take someone who has trouble learning and someday use that person as a college professor.

Beethoven could write music even though he could not hear in later life. Jim Abbott pitches for the California Angels even though he is missing one hand. People who can't see do many things, including downhill skiing.

The great news is that God knows how to take problems and bring good out of them.

Problems stink. It would be fun if all of us could run like a star running back, swim like an olympic star, and sing like the stars at the top of the charts. But we can't. Fortunately there is a loving God who wants to help us use what we have to make a full and satisfying life.

It's hard to imagine what God and you could do together.

> *"And we know that in all things God works for the good of those who love him, who have been called according to his purpose."*
> *Romans 8:28*

Keep thinking

1. What do you have trouble doing that you would like to do better?
2. What is the first step you might take to make that dream come true?
3. What gifts do you think God has given you?

My Parents Embarrass Me

Dad wore that dumb hat. The black one with the ear flaps. Thank goodness he didn't put the flaps down and look like a total dork.

Linda could feel her face heat up when her father came through the door. She was sure everyone could see her blush. Linda had sternly warned her father that when he came to the meeting at school, he wasn't to wear the hat he's had since she was born.

"I'm glad you made it, Dad," Linda said as she shuffled over to stand by his side. "Why don't you slip the hat off and stuff it in your pocket?"

"It's freezing out there," he replied. "If I hadn't worn this hat, my head would be frozen by now."

Almost every kid has felt this way at one time or another about a parent. Maybe your mother has worn a pair of boots that looked like something from the Boer War. Or your dad told a joke to your friends and no one laughed. And you wanted to die.

It isn't just a young person's imagination. Most of us embarrass each other sometime. Every once in a while a teenager does something and his or her parents feel terrible, too. Like when the kid left his underwear on the table inside the front door and company came by. Or when the teacher called to talk about a teenager's bad behavior at school. What about the young person who got a mohawk haircut before discussing it with his parents?

Before parents and teenagers embarrass each other nearly to death, there are a few things we should remember. To begin with, most kids love their parents. They don't like to say so, but if you ask them to write down how they feel, the word *love* shows up sooner or later.

Their love is one of the reasons they are embarrassed. They want their parents to act and look the best they can. Teenagers are proud of their parents and don't want anyone to think they are nerds.

Unfortunately some teenagers worry too much about how their parents will come across. Let your parents be your parents. Short, tall, fat, skinny, quiet, talkative, soft-spoken, loud, snappy dresser, frumpy dresser, wide tie or narrow—let your parents be your parents.

You know how you feel when your parents tell you to change your shirt or sit up straight. That really ticks you off. Your parents feel the same way when you try to tell them to buy designer jeans or to turn off their music tapes.

Teenagers usually love their parents. Out of that love young people can also show mutual respect. Let your parents be your parents. You know you are growing up when you accept your parents exactly as they are.

> *"Each of you must respect his mother and father."*
>
> Leviticus 19:3

Keep thinking

1. What are a few of the things you like about your parents?
2. When did you last thank God for your parents?

Living Your Faith in School

What is the best way to live your Christian faith in school? First, there are some things you should *never* do. These are some ways you should *not* show your faith:

♦ *Never* stand up at the lunch table, take your glass of water and sprinkle everyone's food. It just isn't that holy.

♦ *Never* tell the principal you are praying that God will give him more hair.

♦ *Never* tell your history teacher that God has told you to skip the final exam.

♦ *Never* tell the coach that the word "push-ups" does not appear in the Bible.

♦ *Never* ask your English teacher if you can take up an offering for a new skateboard.

♦ *Never* wear a necktie that lights up and reads, "Repent, the end is near."

Now you know what not to do. But what can you do in a positive way to live like a Christian? Let's look at a few simple reminders.

Hold on to your biblical values. Cheating, stealing, lying, and drugging are not part of your Christian life. As a teen, you will meet other young people who do those things and maybe do them often. As Christians, our first and most important goal is to act like believers in Jesus Christ. That won't always be easy. But Christian behavior and Christian attitudes will see you through some really tough spots.

Treat others with love. You don't have to show off your Christianity. Care about others. Be sincere. Say things that will make others feel good about themselves. Be upbeat. Don't knock everybody and grouch about everything in school. You know God is in charge.

Talk to God about it. Keep in touch so you don't lose sight of who is really important. You can't afford to feel disconnected from the heavenly Father. Conversations with God can be open, friendly, and helpful.

Have an attitude of thankfulness. Be grateful. Each of us has many gifts from God and it's healthy to admit how fortunate we are. No one needs to live a grumpy Christian life. When the time and place is right, you might let someone else know how good God has been to you.

There are many ways to live out the Christian life. These are merely starters. They all begin with the desire: "I *want to* keep my Christian commitment while I go to school." That attitude helps keep your head screwed on right.

> *"In the same way, let your light shine before men, that they may see your good deeds and praise your Father in heaven."*
>
> *Matthew 5:16*

Keep thinking

1. Do your friends know you are a Christian? How do they know that?
2. What are a few of the Christian values most important to you?

When I Get Depressed

"This is the way it happens to me," Brian said, moving his hands as he spoke. "When I feel three or four things going wrong all at once, I think everything is falling in on me. That's when I decide to give up.

"I go to my room, close the door, and refuse to feel anything. I shut my body down. I shut my brain down and I just get depressed."

Brian's experience is quite common. People of all ages let themselves get depressed when too many things are going wrong. Some teenagers often choose depression because their lives are changing rapidly. New friends, new classes, body growth, hair sprouting out, voice changing, legs getting longer—it's a lot to deal with all at once.

One day you can feel good about all the changes, but the next day you feel terrible. Sometimes, when you get tired of the emotional roller coaster, you may decide to get off. Depressing is a way of getting off the thrill ride.

Life can be rough. Sooner or later it's a miserable trip for most of us. When the problems pile up, we each have to make a choice. Do you want to handle each problem one at a time? Or do you want to sit in a corner and stick your head under your arm? If you stick your head under your arm, that means you want to drop out of the battle for a while.

We hear someone say, "I can't help it. I'm just depressed." That person is depressed, but most of us can do something about it. It's like someone standing in a lake with water up to the knees and saying, "I can't help it, my feet are just wet." The person's correct. His or her feet are wet *but* it can be helped. For one thing, the person could choose to walk out of the water.

During the teen years there is plenty of opportunity to go in the depression dumper. But young people who decide to face their problems get a great deal more out of life. Those who are in the habit of getting down find these years much rougher.

For most, depression is *not* an uncontrollable mood that sweeps over us. It isn't a ghost hiding behind a tree waiting to jump out and eat us. Usually depression is something we do to ourselves. And there is something we can do about it. However, for some people, it can be difficult to get out alone. Then it's time to go for help.

To begin with, you can ask God to help you have a good attitude. Let God show you how to get the most out of life and how to put the most into life. God would rather see you open faced and involved than pouting and sulking.

> *"So Ahab went home, sullen and angry because Naboth the Jezreelite had said, 'I will not give you the inheritance of my fathers.' He lay on his bed sulking and refused to eat."*
>
> 1 Kings 21:4

Keep thinking

1. What kind of things are likely to put you in the depression dumper?
2. What do you do that helps cheer you up?

Up in Smoke

A group of junior high students told me how they viewed smoking at their school. They said not many students smoked in their community, but it seemed to follow a pattern:

1. There seemed to be more smokers in junior high than senior high.
2. They saw it as a form of rebellion—not against their parents but against the school administration.
3. Most often the smokers were the students who were beginning to drop out. Their behavior was anti-social and anti-school.

Not every group or community is the same. This may not be the way you see the young people where you live. But there could be some truth to how they see the situation.

There has always been something daring about smoking. Even the fire involved increases the risk, and for some people that danger makes it more attractive. All of us look for something in life that is a little exciting and out of the ordinary. When we were children we climbed trees or jumped off garage roofs. Now some teens turn to smoking.

Lots of young people think nothing really bad ever will happen to them. Scares about cancer or becoming addicted to nicotine or pot don't affect many young people. They even chew tobacco and insist it can't hurt their teeth, cheeks, gums, or throats.

Trying to frighten or educate teens about the facts is usually not effective in changing their minds. Like people of other ages, teenagers have to change their own minds.

Smoking is even more attractive because it gets teachers, parents, principals, doctors, and some police all excited. A few teenagers love to see adults get angry, raise their voices, and threaten young people. The more adults become frustrated and jump up and down, the more some teenagers smoke. That's one of the games we enjoy playing.

If a young person wants to sneak behind a building and steal a few puffs when given the chance, there probably aren't many ways to stop him or her. Teens will find a way to smoke, if they want to. That's the fact for most people.

When you were a child your parents merely took the matches away, sat you in a corner and didn't let you have any brownies after dinner. It isn't that simple now that you are a teen.

Most young people wise up when it comes to smoking. A few don't and get hurt. Those who gain some wisdom early are really the fortunate ones.

> "Blessed is the man who finds wisdom, the man who gains understanding."
>
> *Proverbs 3:13*

Keep thinking

1. How many teenagers do you see smoking?
2. Why do you or your friends smoke?
3. What do you think you will do about smoking?

Her Chest
Is Too Small

She stands in front of the mirror and extends her arms. Tightly she locks her fingers together and begins her "tension" exercises. Her hope is to build up her muscles so she will develop a large chest, or more precisely, big breasts.

When many girls become teenagers and their bodies begin to mature, breast size is one of the first questions they have. They don't wonder if their hands will be large enough or their feet the right size. They want to know how they will look in a sweater or in a bathing suit.

Girls are smart. They know what the big emphasis is on television and in the movies. They understand what boys laugh about as they look at magazines and commercials. Jokes and graffiti are often focused on breasts.

But the really smart girls soon start to see how crazy all of that is. How would you like to know that a boy liked you only because of your body size? He didn't care about your personality or your mind or your values or your hopes. Would you want to date a guy just because he liked your chest? If he does, what kind of a date is that likely to become?

It's OK to worry about your breasts. After all, you can worry about anything you want. There are thin girls who think they're fat. There are tall girls who think they are too tall. Girls with red hair want to have brunette and those who are brunette want to be blonde. Straight hair wants to be curly and curly wants to be straight. You can worry about anything you want, and you probably will.

Some girls will wear pads to look larger. A few will get implants. Too many will worry about their chest size from the time they are 11 years old until they are 73. Maybe people like to worry.

The fact is that in your early teens you can't know what your breast size will be. You may remain small for years and suddenly have a spurt of growth. You could grow rapidly the first few years and quit growing just as quickly.

At some time chest size bothers most girls. If it upsets you, remember a few things you already know:

1. Aim to be a caring, loving person, and not someone with big body parts.
2. Boys who giggle about girls' chests aren't very mature.
3. Never aim to "catch" guys with your body.
4. God tells us that it is the inside of a person that really counts. The outside isn't who the person is.

"The Lord does not look at the things man looks at. Man looks at the outward appearance, but the Lord looks at the heart."

1 Samuel 16:7

Keep thinking

1. Have you ever stopped to thank God for your appearance? Not that your appearance is better than someone else's, but have you given thanks for your own hair and eyes and shoulders?
2. What is there about your personality and attitude that you would like to keep improving?

My Parents Don't Like My Friends

When Daniel came to Kirk's house, he made himself at home. Daniel would sit in Kirk's dad's favorite chair and loop one leg over the chair arm. He liked to chew nuts, crack them loudly, and spit the shells into his hands. Daniel was a noisy, constant talker. Whenever the cat came into the room, Daniel would lunge at the poor creature, sending it scrambling out of sight.

Kirk's friend was bold, outgoing, and a little risky. Though Daniel only stayed a few minutes, he made all of Kirk's family nervous until Daniel was safely out the door.

"Are you sure Daniel is good for you?" Kirk's father asked when they were alone.

"What's wrong with Daniel?" Kirk defended his friend.

"Well, he has a lot of energy. I just wondered if he's the kind of guy who gets into trouble."

After that Kirk didn't feel comfortable letting Daniel into his house. A couple of times Kirk asked his friend to wait on the porch while he darted inside to pick up something.

Kirk felt hurt trying to hide his friend so his parents wouldn't get upset. Finally he decided to take some action. He figured it was worth a try.

"Do me a big favor," Kirk told Daniel. "Try to treat the cat gently. My parents treat that cat like a kid. Oh, and keep your legs off the furniture. That's a big deal around my house. You and my parents are going to get along great."

The next day Kirk caught his father standing in the kitchen and told him, "Daniel's coming over tonight. Wait until you see how he acts this time. He's still a little noisy, but remember Uncle Ralph isn't exactly a mummy himself."

Later Daniel arrived. Before going to the basement to shoot pool, he sat for a few minutes with Kirk's family. Daniel sat up straight like a store mannequin. He waved at the cat but didn't grab the creature.

"Well, let's go shoot some pool," Kirk said after a few minutes of small talk.

As Daniel stood to leave the room, he said, "Hey, I really like your Chinese picture, Mr. Rawlson."

"Well thank you, Daniel. Actually it's Mexican," replied Kirk's father. "We picked it up on a trip last winter."

"Chinese, Mexican, I knew it was something like that," Daniel said as he hurried out of the room.

As Kirk passed through the doorway he looked back to see his dad give him a grin and a big wink.

Kirk wanted to find a way to make peace between his friend and his family. He was willing to work on both sides to bring about harmony.

"Blessed are the peacemakers, for they will be called sons of God."

Matthew 5:9

Keep thinking

1. Do you have a friend your parents don't appreciate? What is your parents' point of view? What is your friend's point of view?
2. How could you help your parents and your friend change just a little?

Split Parents

The divorce rate has been increasing rapidly over the past few years. Nearly everyone knows someone who is divorced or whose parents are thinking about getting divorced. Perhaps your parents are. What happens to the kids? They probably live with one parent and the other parent lives across town, across the state or who knows where. Usually kids in divorced families live with their mothers, but some live with their fathers.

Divorce is often tough on young people. Their feelings race around like characters on a video game. They have hot and cold rushes of love, hate, confusion, self-pity, loneliness, vengeance, fear, hope, and even guilt.

Sometimes they play the blame game. Was it their father's fault? Did their mother mess up? A few teens blame themselves for the big split. And what about God? Where was God when all of this battling was going on?

In the long run the blame game only hurts us. There is no point in picking out someone to blame and spending the rest of your life hating him or her. Someone messed up. Maybe several people messed up. And it's true that their mistakes have brought pain into your life. Nobody can argue with that.

Have you ever met kids of divorced parents who are bitter about their world? Nothing ever goes right, according to them. They go through life with a sarcastic growl; they throw rocks at squirrels, kick over trash baskets, and run their VCRs backwards. Everything stinks, according to them, and they have trouble finding anything good to talk about.

If their world is ever going to straighten out, they must forgive their parents. That's asking a lot, especially after what some parents have done. But the lives of kids from divorced families may always be a tiny ball of pain until they let go and forgive the people who have hurt them.

Maybe you are one of those people. Forgive your parents so you can enjoy tomorrow. Forgive them so you can loosen up and be happy. Forgive them so you can spend your energy on things you like. Forgive them so you can open up and feel free from hate. Forgive them so you won't have a heavy weight around your neck as you go through school.

God has been generous at forgiving us. We can be grateful and forgive our parents.

> *"Be kind and compassionate to one another, forgiving each other, just as in Christ God forgave us."*
>
> *Ephesians 4:32*

Keep thinking

1. Do you blame your parents for something that has happened in your life?
2. Would you like to forgive them now?

What about
My Fantasies?

At age 16 Kellen was a tormented person. Since he was 11 or 12, he had thought of all kinds of sexual fantasies. Kellen had imagined himself kissing pretty girls. Some of them were television stars and others were the girls he knew at school.

As a youth he had also dreamed of some unusual relationships with teachers. When Kellen discovered magazines with pictures of nude women, he found himself thinking a great deal about those women.

The biggest problem was that Kellen began to believe he was weird because of the things he thought. He became depressed and started to stay by himself a great deal. Above all, he felt terribly guilty.

Kellen could have been spared a lot of guilt if someone had only told him, "Kellen, you're normal." He was no monster. He didn't have a warped or sick mind. He needed to know a few facts about people.

1. *Most of us think strange things.* Not everyone thinks about the same weird things, but we are all capable of showing strange movies in our minds. We imagine ourselves as ship captains, slave drivers, great lovers, billionaires, kings, queens, and astronauts.

Sometimes we dream about these things on purpose. Other times the little movies sneak in without warning. We all need to know we are normal.

2. *We ought to exercise some control.* If we live in a dream world all the time, we might be getting a bit too far from reality. Most of us could do a little better. If you

let your brain run as wild as it can every day, you can have trouble getting it back in the corral.

Teenagers can talk to their minds. They can just say, "Hey, you're getting too weird too often. Let's calm down." A brain's life isn't entirely its own. We feel better if we boss our gray matter around once in a while.

3. *Pump good stuff in.* There is plenty of opportunity to think wacko. Every evening on TV we can watch heads being ripped off, clothes torn to shreds, grandmothers thrown down stairs, husbands cheating on their wives. Newspapers, television, and videos supply us with tons of crazy things.

The Bible tells us to pump some fresh air into our brain. Think of ways to help people. Dream of a good ball game. Remember a great friend. Have a short conversation with God. Plan a trip. Call someone and laugh awhile.

All of us visit fantasies, but we don't have to live there.

> *"Finally, brothers, whatever is true, whatever is noble, whatever is right, whatever is pure, whatever is lovely, whatever is admirable—if anything is excellent or praiseworthy—think about such things."*
>
> Philippians 4:8

Keep thinking

1. Are there some shows that are more likely to give you fantasies, nightmares, or leave you depressed? Which ones?
2. When you take control over your brain, what do you do to change your mood?

When Dating Starts

"In my school," Chad explained, "dating is mostly short-term stuff. You might walk around the mall with a girl for a couple of hours and have a Coke. There aren't many places you can go without wheels. If a couple decides to go steady, that only lasts a few weeks."

Dating is a big topic during the teen years. Not many people do it often, but they talk about it a great deal.

It can be fun, but dating has its headaches, too. The rush to start dating can easily backfire. Let it happen slowly and naturally. Worrying about dating or forcing it too early can lead to problems you wish you never had.

There are kids who date only once or twice during the seventh through the 12th grades and some who don't date at all. But when they get to college or on the job, dates seem to come running from every direction. Others date no one until they meet Mr. or Miss Right. Then they fall like a rock, marry that person, and have a fantastic relationship.

Dating is enjoyable for those who handle it right, but it's far from the end of the world. You might find that hard to believe at 13, but keep it in mind during the next few years.

It's smart to maintain good communication with both boys and girls. If you don't, it's easy to forget how to be natural around members of the opposite sex. Go places in groups, work on projects together, join youth groups, grab a well-rounded life so you will feel comfortable with anyone. People who hide from the opposite sex often develop an awkwardness that is hard to overcome later.

Make yourself a pledge that you will not envy others. If Mark and Staci date twice a week, that's their business. You don't need to be like anyone else. Be excited about being you.

Pledge number two: Be happy to be patient. There are plenty of things to get involved in and lots of activities to enjoy. Make the most of those. Only dodos sit around waiting for the phone to ring.

Have you ever met a young person who lived to date? He or she found self-worth only in going out. When the phone didn't ring, the person became depressed, disgusted, and dumpy.

Tell yourself you are too smart for that. You will be the patient kind. You are in no hurry to force something you might regret. And you are certainly not going to let it get you twisted out of shape.

"A man's wisdom gives him patience."
                                            Proverbs 19:11

Keep thinking

1. What activities do you enjoy?
2. How many of your friends date?

Could I Be Gay?

Todd liked to spend an evening now and then in the kitchen. Baking a cake or whipping together a few pans of cookies was a great deal of fun for this teenager. Todd never bragged about his hobby and was afraid to share the baked goods with friends. He simply put his cookies in the jar with his mother's and didn't say a word to other guys.

Shelly enjoyed playing baseball and she was good at it. She could outrun most of the boys and bat better than anyone in the sixth grade. But becoming a teenager was a serious problem to the athletic Shelly. If she was a "tomboy," she wasn't sure she could grow into a young lady, have dates, and be accepted.

Even her girlfriends called her "Butch," and that worried her. Shelly didn't want to be a boy; she merely wanted to be a girl who was a good athlete. Now she was afraid of being left out and misunderstood.

Schools are packed with Todds and Shellys. Boys who appreciate creating and drawing. Girls who would rather hammer nails than paint their own. Later in life those activities are better accepted. There are men who like to do needlepoint and women who enjoy working on cars.

But when you are young, you often wonder if you are a girl who wants to be a boy, or a boy who wants to be a girl. And some days you begin to think you might be part girl and part boy or something.

Don't be fooled by the little things. Keep these facts in mind:

♦ An apron never made a boy gay.

- A basketball never made a girl a lesbian.
- It's all right for a boy to think another boy is good looking.
- It's healthy for a girl to want another girl to hug her.
- Some of the prettiest girls in the world have short haircuts.
- Girls can drive trucks and boys can play violins.

Feel free to be yourself. You are made in God's image; both boys and girls are made in the image of God. Don't be afraid to do what really interests you.

God created voices so both males and females could sing. God formed mountains for both boys and girls to climb and enjoy. Pick up a rock and see what it says on the bottom. Is there a note from God that says, "For boys only"? If there is no message there, a girl can throw the rock across the creek just as well as a boy can.

None of these things ever made a boy gay or a girl a lesbian.

> "Then God said, 'Let us make man in our image, in our likeness.'"
>
> Genesis 1:26

Keep thinking

1. What do you like to do that other people think is weird?
2. Have you ever thanked God for making you exactly the way you are? Would this be a good time to do that?

A Big Cheer
for Deodorants

The next time you begin thanking God for beautiful days, good parents, and rippling streams, you might want to throw in one forgotten gift. Thank God for great deodorants. Without those little body fresheners, we might pass out in the classroom.

Sweating is a wholesome, healthy process that all of us need. God put a thermostat in your body much like the one in your house. When your body gets too warm, your brain picks up the message. It then kicks on your sweat glands, telling them to cool down your body.

The sweat itself doesn't cool down our bodies. Like when you first step out of a swimming pool, it's the evaporation of the water that does the job.

We have sweat glands on most parts of our bodies, but certain areas have an extra supply. The bottoms of our feet, the palms of our hands, and naturally our armpits have large sweat glands.

On hot and humid days it's easy to see how much we sweat. The temperature and humidity are high and often we are more active. Your clothes get damp and the body odor can almost make your eyes sting, especially if you are indoors.

But don't let the cold days fool you. We sweat even when we can't see it or feel it.

Baths and showers go a long way toward solving the odor problem. We can wash off the body particles left by sweating. A deodorized soap helps. We then top it off with an effective deodorant.

If you keep deodorant in your school locker, you will have some help in emergencies. Most of us feel more confident if we don't have to worry about smelling like burnt rubber.

Much of our time will be spent in rooms crowded with other teenagers or family members. It's awfully nice if we are pleasant to be around.

At first many young people overdo the deodorant bit. (So do some adults.) But you will soon discover what works for you.

Showers were harder to get during Bible times, but people were still careful to avoid being offensive. A quick shot of perfume or deodorant made life more pleasant for everyone.

"Pleasing is the fragrance of your perfumes."
Song of Solomon 1:3

Keep thinking

1. Do you have some hints for personal grooming and cleanliness?
2. How do you schedule time for personal hygiene?

How Do You Say No?

When someone offers you a few puffs on a joint—"just to get a sample of what marijuana tastes like" —how will you be able to say you don't want any? How will you make the person realize that you want to take the clearheaded approach to life? How do you say no?

There are several ways to do it.

♦ Tell the person you have mouth rot and other people can catch it if you share the same cigarette.

♦ Explain that your uncle in Bangor, Maine, has offered you one million dollars if you never try drugs.

♦ Say you might try the joint if the person would first eat a sample of the bat brains and pig saliva you have prepared.

♦ Assure the person you would like to, but the last time you smoked one your seven-foot-tall brother found the person who gave it to you and twisted his left arm off.

♦ Ask if you can share the joint with your next-door neighbor, a police officer named Bruno.

Of course, none of these is really the best answer. The best reply is a short, direct no. Don't waste your time with a polite, "No, thank you, I'd rather not." Don't give a cloudy "Not now." Don't give a tentative, "Maybe later." The last thing we want to do is give a drug pusher any encouragement. Never make the pusher think you haven't made up your mind.

If a pusher—even a friend who is a pusher—thinks he or she can sway you, you might be open to further contact.

He or she will stick with you like gum on a shoe. When someone invites you to smoke marijuana, he or she is pushing the stuff even if you don't have to pay for it.

Sooner or later almost everyone is offered dope, cocaine, crack, and even worse. Smart teenagers make up their minds early about how they will react. If you decide to say no, God has promised that you will be given help to resist the stuff. None of us is alone. But we have to make the decision. God won't do that for us.

Tell God how you feel about drugs. Ask God to help you stick by your decision. The two of you make a fantastic team.

> *"No temptation has seized you except what is common to man. And God is faithful; he will not let you be tempted beyond what you can bear. But when you are tempted, he will also provide a way out so that you can stand up under it."*
>
> *1 Corinthians 10:13*

Keep thinking

1. Are there drugs in your neighborhood? In your school?
2. How do you feel about using drugs?
3. What would you say if drugs were offered to you?

Fickle Faith

By now you have heard lots of the Bible stories, especially if you grew up in church. They were good and even helpful, but at your age it's time to move on. You can't talk about someone else's faith forever. You are mature enough to ask serious questions for yourself.

It was easier before. Most of us were pulled around, told when to sit in what chair, and then told what to believe. You probably believed what the church believed, what your parents believed, what your teacher believed. We like to shake our heads and agree with everyone as often as we can. But you aren't a child anymore. Becoming a teenager means you must find your personal faith. What do you believe?

Don't be surprised if you have some bad days with your faith. You want to ask questions, to push, pull, and make sure you understand. Belief in Jesus Christ is a serious commitment and needs some first-class thought. Maybe you asked Jesus into your life years ago, or possibly you are close to making that decision. Either way, it can be a bumpy road for a while. Don't let it throw you.

If you have questions about God or Jesus or the Bible, you deserve good answers. There aren't answers for everything. We need to know that, too. At some point we need to take a jump by faith and decide to follow Christ. But where answers are available, we want to ask to find out.

Today you may find it easy to believe. Tomorrow you might wonder if you believe anything. That's normal and happens to full-fledged adults. During the roller coaster early teens your faith could be a little more fickle. With so many changes going on, your mind is often in a whirl anyway.

As you sift through what you hear, read, and see, make a decision for yourself. Ask Jesus to come into your life. Then believe that he will. That's the only way anyone comes to Jesus Christ.

As you investigate the subject of personal faith, you might see the roller coaster begin to level off. As you resolve each question in your own mind, the ride gets smoother. Then one day you realize that you are a Christian because you want to be one. That day move from a fickle faith into a firm one.

> " 'Yes, Lord,' she told him, 'I believe that you are the Christ, the Son of God, who was to come into the world.' "
>
> *John 11:27*

Keep thinking

1. What convinced you to believe in Jesus Christ?
2. How has knowing Christ helped you?